Three Hours to Burn a Body

Poems on Travel

Three Hours to Burn a Body

Poems on Travel

Suzanne Roberts

Cherry Grove Collections

Published by Cherry Grove Collections
P.O. Box 541106
Cincinnati, OH 45254-1106

ISBN: 9781936370375
LCCN: 2011927990

Poetry Editor: Kevin Walzer
Business Editor: Lori Jareo

Visit us on the web at www.cherry-grove.com

Cover photo by Lucy Gledhill
Cover design by Suzanne Roberts
Author photo by Sholeh Wolpé

My gratitude to the editors of the following journals, in which versions of these poems first appeared:

Alligator Juniper: "The Mongolian Disco"

Atlanta Review: "Devotion"

Diverse City: reprinted "Devotion"

Drunken Boat: "The Truth"

EcoCollective Journal: "Animal Market" and "El Pozo"

Fourth River: "Poultry Stall," "At the Café," "Almost Dawn," "Jungle Lodge," and "Almost Somewhere"

The MacGuffin: "The Hutong," "The Road," and "Throat Singing"

Matador: "3AM"

Mead: "In the Train Station"

Melusine: "This Girl's Life"

Mountain Gazette: "The Syntax of Gravity"

National Geographic Traveler: "Three Hours to Burn a Body"

Palestine Chronicle: "A Call to Prayer"

Poetry of Travel: "Almost Dawn"

Quay: "Homestay" and "At the Café"

The Sacramento News & Review: "Unrequited Love"

Short Poem: "After Midnight"

Terrain: "Incan Wall"

Tonopah Review: "Earth-Bound"

Valparaiso Poetry Review: "Rain"

My gratitude to the Wordy Girls, Kim Wyatt, Liv Spikes, and Janet Smith, for writerly advice, support, and friendship. And many thanks to Kevin Walzer and Lori Jareo for all the work they do to bring poetry into the world.

Table of Contents

For the people across the globe
who welcomed me into their worlds

And for my adventurous traveling companions:
Sandra Breylinger, Sholeh Wolpé, & Tracy Young

And for my travel partner for life: Thomas Greene

I. Crossings

"One's destination is never a place, but rather a new way of looking at things."

—*Henry Miller*

Midnight in the Plaza

Granada, Nicaragua

They teeter across the cobblestones
in silver platforms, pink halters,
sequined dresses. They flutter false eyelashes,
ask, *You want girl tonight? You want me?*
They gather on the corner, across from the church,
where artisans sell ceramics earlier in the day.
Rather than shout *cerámica* the girls call out
chicas. A gray-haired man passes them,
slows his pace. He wears the tourist uniform—
the zip-off rain pants, floppy sun hat,
Teva sandals. I will him to pass them by.
They try harder, call, *Have me tonight?*
I think, Please don't. They are 11 or 12,
young enough to be his granddaughters, dressed
in their mothers' ill-fitting evening wear,
the heavy eyeliner, blue shadow, red lipstick,
a game of dress-up. In another country.
As the man moves in to choose,
he notices my watching, turns to me, says,
"I wasn't going to. It's not my thing.
It's one night, but then the next thing
you know, you're taking care of the family.
You're buying Grandpa his teeth. For these girls,

it's hitting the jackpot." He crosses the street
but circles back around under the streetlamps,
passing the church. We had ridden horses
by this church in the morning, little girls
in school dresses climbed the chain-link fence
of the churchyard. They clung to the wire
like Christmas tree ornaments, waved to us
as we rode past. They giggled when we waved back,
their shouts, *hola, hola,* echoed off the cobblestone.

Away

León, Nicaragua

A wooden cross hangs on the yellow wall.
Cockroaches scurry under the bed, along
the red tile floor. The ceiling fan squeaks.
The fountain outside, a mosaic of water, of night.
Window shades, broken, clatter. Palms rustle.
The television picks up an American station.
Spanish subtitles scroll along the screen.
A plane circles Boston, the landing gear stuck.
They will run out their fuel, control a crash landing.
I reach for the remote, turn it off. As you enter me,
you tell me, I am yours—it's your lie. Mine
is to pretend I'm here, rather than thinking
about how someone else will be making love when I die.

After the Storm

Little Corn Island, Nicaragua

The hotel boy sifts through the mounds
of brown seaweed, white sand. The Caribbean,
storm tossed. The boy throws plastic spoons,
water bottles and caps, pens and toothbrushes
into a bin, tidying up the storm-strewn beach
for us, the tourists.

I watch him, then offer to help.
He asks if I'm sure. I nod, he smiles.
We work in silence, sorting through coconuts
and seeds, pulling out torn flip-flops, straws,
traffic pylons, Penzoil containers,
disposable razors, syringes, an IV bag.

My scream surprises me: a drowned rat,
the fur matted with salt and sand.
The claws curled, the head reaching up,
as if swimming through death's rigidity.
The eyes open wide, the sharp yellow teeth
biting the absence of air.

The boy leaves the rat in the sand,
works around it. He tells me that it's time

to carry the garbage to the boat. That
it was nice meeting me. We shake hands.
He hoists the bin to his shoulder, takes the path
through the jungle, disappears.

I return to my towel, watch a coconut
wobble up shore with the rising tide,
rolling into the water each time
the white curtain retreats.
Up and back down like Sisyphus' rock,
returning sea to sand to sea.

Haircutting Ceremony

The Kuna Yala Islands

1.

The caged pig hovers over the water, unable to turn around in her wire pen. A woman stands on the dock, holding quivering fish by their tails —the scales like stacked coins, the green eyes like marbles. The gills fan at the useless air. We pay the arrival taxes, walk through the narrow and treeless streets, pass the thatched roofs, the corrugated tin. Lanterns burn yellow in the filtered light.

2.

Children smile and wave, call the only Spanish words they know, *Hola, hola. Nombre? País?* They run past, their laughter ringing through the maze of streets.

3.

An albino girl runs from a group of older boys. She wears the colorful *molas*, beads crawling up her pinkish skin. She is sunburned, mottled with insect bites—the pink flares like fireworks splitting the blankness of sky. They tease her, reach for her budding chest. Her stringy blond hair hangs from under an orange head scarf. The blue eyes transparent. The laughter, the mocking—the language of different we all understand.

4.

I am waved into the tented town square. I duck under the canvas. The darkness knits over the outside world. The backlit sky disappears. Only the tips of cigarettes burn orange and the flicker of candles, the wax melting into empty beer cans. Smoke hovers like a memory. A man plays a hand flute in the dark corner. Another shakes a gourd of beads.

5.

The elders unfold themselves from the low wooden benches, pour *Seco Herrerano* into split coconut shells. They line up on the dirt floor, clutching their rum. They sing "*Woo-woo-woo-woo,*" shuffle along the floor, polished smooth by bare feet. They stoop their shoulders, come together, raise their coconuts, drink. The song, *Idomalando*, a chant for health. The dance, an ancient ritual I cannot name.

6.

The painted and pierced women drink and smoke and gossip on their side of the tent. They sit arm and arm, swaying on their benches, giggling to one another like schoolgirls, leaning into each other, laughing over the din of drinking. The patterned *molas*, skirts, head scarves, geometric beading glimmer blue, yellow, purple—sequins of light interrupting the darkness.

7.

A man tosses his cigarette onto the dirt floor, puts it out with his bare foot. He pours rum into a coconut bowl, comes to me with this offering. The family, our translator explains in Spanish, wants everyone to enjoy the ceremony. I hold the rum with both hands. It burns into my stomach, a fire spreading into the limbs.

8.

Dizzy, I get up from the wood plank on the floor, stumble out of the tent into the gauzy light. I pass an old woman. A gold ring hangs from her septum, the orange make-up blazed along triangular cheekbones, down the length of her nose. She sucks hard on a cigarette, sways toward me, points at my face, says, "*Borracha.*" Drunk. The smoke hangs in the air like a question. I nod, not knowing if she means me or herself. Or both.

9.

I return to the tent, wait for the girl to enter, imagine the sheared hair falling like rain, signaling her passage into womanhood. She never appears. Maybe the ritual is held in secret, the twelve-year-old girl crying as she watches her childhood spiral to the dusty ground. I don't have the language to ask.

The Truth

Amazonas, Colombia

I follow the guide into the clearing,
leave the embryonic forest,
the green canopy, a quilt of shadow.
Blue butterflies as big as my hand
flit into the light. The ellipses
of scorched grass crackle underneath
our rubber boots. The noontime sun burns
in the sky, the air no longer burdened
with the weight of water, green vines,
and dreams. Cows wander across
the yellowed grass. White egrets follow.
Saw-chewed stumps of grandmother ceibas
hide among the banana trees, the plantains.
Muy feo, I say. *Y triste*. So very ugly. And sad.
Es la verdad, our guide says, It's the truth.
Pero la gente no puede comer los árboles.
But the people cannot eat the trees.

At the Café

Cusco, Perú

I order another glass of red wine,
though it comes from a leather bag,
tastes like burnt skin. No one will ask,
Don't you think you're drinking too much?
Then I'll try a café or coca leaf tea, another
piece of dry lemon cake. Eat it
in the dim and dirty light. Stay
up all night, walk the streets
with the children selling postcards.
No one knowing where I am—
the certain freedom that comes only
with loneliness. The margin between
wanting everything, and wanting
nothing, growing fainter and fainter.

Homestay

Cusco, Perú

Juanna tells me she has seventeen years,
has worked for this family ever since
her new papa married her mama,
didn't want her. Or her sisters.
The family tells me she's lucky.
She cooks and cleans, smiles
with eyes tired of a sightless faith.
She watches the other children
leave for school, go out dancing,
eat meals with me while she waits
until everyone has finished, eats alone
only after washing the dishes.
She listens to the *real* daughter
tell me she wants to visit New York,
because of the glamorous women
of *Sex in the City*. In my broken Spanish,
I tell her not very many American women
are like Carrie Bradshaw or Samantha Jones,
causing her to pout and declare,
"I will never ask you anything else."
She stomps from the room, leaving
her dinner to go cold. I finish
eating alone, and Juanna tells me

she's glad about the women in America,
had believed the same thing.
Then she tells me she's lost
one of her sisters, says,
"We don't know where she is."
Then, "It is so hard to be the oldest."
Juanna leans on her mop, having already
seen with an old woman's eyes.

After Midnight

Cusco, Perú

I wake sometime in the small hours,
within a shadow, terrified.

The sounds back, the blaring taxi horns,
stray dogs barking.

The glow of the streetlamps bleed
into the room. The place forming again—

a bed, a room, a locked door.

Incan Wall

Sacsayhuamán, Perú

Inside the belly of the cave,
a darkness more than metaphor
erases rock walls, ceiling,
ground, me. I find myself

alone in a literal darkness,
in the center of nothing,
realize this cold, dark womb
could be the only fear.

But I emerge, of course—
a light-flooded Andean backdrop,
the undulation of green flickering
before white-haired mountains.

My mother says when she dies,
it could be days before anyone
would find her. Such comfort
in being found still warm.

Almost Dawn

Lima, Perú

Madonna's "Papa Don't Preach" blares
from the taxi's radio. Hotel workers
wait on the corners for buses in the gray smear
of dawn. Stilettoed young women spill
from discos, huddle together, whisper
to each other behind cupped palms.
The Hollywood Casino flashes orange
with dancing lights. An old woman
pushes a small broken boy between the lanes
of traffic. The taxi stops at a light, the woman
knocks on the car window, holds out her hand,
a small, dirty nest. The streetlight turns
from red to green, glows in a field
of fog. We accelerate past, leave them
behind. The driver asks where I'm going.
I've said *aeropuerto*, but now, I say *airport*,
even though I know he means, which country?
I pretend not to speak Spanish, pretend
not to understand.

El Pozo

Orellana, Ecuador
for Pamela Ramírez

An oil worker stands in front
of the early morning flames.
A smokestack penetrates a sky
swollen with water, an impending
aguacero, black rain falling
on a tired patch of red earth,
stinging a downriver jungle
with watery fire. A girl missing
an eye looks toward an inherited sky.

Animal Market

Saquisilí, Ecuador

A lamb is tied to the top of a bus,
bleats into the wind in terror.
Guinea pigs scatter and squeal
in a wire cage, saved

For special occasions, a delicacy.
We have tried them, curled
crispy on a plate, claws and all.
Men with sticks prod screaming pigs,

Piled into the bed of a pickup truck.
I take a picture, a man turns,
sticks his tongue out at me.
A woman holds a pink-eyed rabbit,

Swings it by the ears.
Another woman walks toward us,
lifts her shirt, shows us
the place where a nipple

Should be, instead a gash, red
as a plum. She holds out her hand,

opens her mouth without sound.

We walk past, no longer looking.

Poultry Stall

Saquisilí, Ecuador

A stout woman holds chickens
upside down, swinging them
by their feet. They do not fight her.
Their almond eyes wide, open
to an inverted world, looking
at nothing. A potential customer
comes by, feels the bodies
under the white feathers, already
meat. While the women negotiate
a fair price, the customer ruffles
her fingers along the bellies.
Still the chickens do nothing,
as we often do, resigned already
to being dead.

Almost Somewhere

Quito, Ecuador

Armed guards keep out the man selling
sunglasses, a woman, exposing an injured
foot, begging for change. The travelers here
can rest assured, the bullet-proof vests
will keep them from harm. They can exchange
stories—the jungle in Cuyabena, the Galapagos,
tell each other of good eats—Mexican food
in Ecuador, Thai food in Lima, Peru.
They complain of early morning flights, long bus rides,
the burden of malaria pills. The television replays
NFL highlights. The guards stand at the entrance,
so the travelers, all of them almost somewhere,
can eat their waffles in peace.

Crossings

Quito, Ecuador

A small boy and his black puppy
run in front of our bus, cross
the Pan American Highway
One of them makes it across.

Jungle Lodge

Outside Tena, Ecuador

He's come to see you in Ecuador.

You ride busses, motorcycles, hike

to waterfalls. You fuck. You argue.

You ask if he'll apologize. He answers

from underneath the ratty sheet, No way.

So you slam shut the door, write

in your journal, *If you don't say*

you're sorry, Voy a salir, en serio.

The language has bled into your rage.

But seriously, where would you go?

You can't throw yourself from the balcony,

past the baby pineapples, into the muddy river

below just because you're mad, feeling

dramatic. Did you mention it's beautiful here?

The striated grasshopper on the mirror

of the outdoor bathroom, the green river,

snaking through the jungle. The delicate

netting of a mosquito screen, a drenched sky

absent of stars. And a dead yellow parakeet

on the porch, the wings wet, useless with rain.

A Different Kind of Animal

Galapágos Islands, Ecuador

The boat shimmies across the equator
at midnight. We drink Pisco Sours, dance
salsa with the crew. The others throw up
into the sea. We know how to follow the waves,
sway with the boat. The sounds of water,
the aching boards beneath our feet bow and creak.
The first mate turns up the music, drowning out
the sounds of sickness. The captain has one eye
on the black horizon, the other on my friend Sandra.
The bartender tries to teach me to dance—impossible
even on static ground. He demonstrates, then laughs,
Tiene algunos problemas con las piernas.
There must be some problem with your legs.
They pretend they aren't married, don't have
four or six children each. Like the boobies kicking up
their webbed blue feet, showing off impressive wing spans,
our small crew does their best to dance their way
into our hearts, our pants. It's almost enough.
Like the female birds, we act demure, encourage
their dance, but try to stay one step ahead
of them. They know the dance well—next week
will bring another boatload of tourists, more drinks and dancing.
More lonely ladies—we have seen the cook's photographs.

When we showed him our pictures of the mating pairs

of albatross, he showed us his—not photographs of birds

but women tourists, mostly in bathing suits, some

dancing, captured on his digital screen. He smiled

a toothless grin. Sandra pointed to her camera, told him—

her Spanish better than mine—the albatross mate for life.

Yes, he answered, there's procreation. Then there's fucking.

Unrequited Love

Volcán Pacaya, Guatemala

The earth's breath, her groan.
El anillo de fuego—
lips parted, whispering flames.
If only my skin tasted
like the coral glow.

The Stranger

Tepotzlán, México

A Jesus mannequin hangs on the wall.
His painted face, pained. Red droplets
skirt his brow under the wire crown.
The oversized blue eyes to the sky,
chipped fingers clasped in prayer.
An old man in the front row kneels,
his furrowed brow rests on the tips
of his calloused fingers. His graying hair,
sweat-flattened, the wide-brimmed hat
on the pew next to him.

Sweat slides down my back,
sticks my thighs to the scratched
wooden pew. I can't stop myself
from staring. The old man looks up
at the plaster statue. His eyes murky
with cataracts. I try to imagine
his world, gauzy behind a white veil.
I can't imagine his faith, try to
assign him some kind of shame
but know it is all mine.

This Girl's Life

Bristol Avenue, Blackpool, England

Take Jack Smith, who got his sister
pregnant. Everyone knew. He left
for the war. She stayed home,
listening to the radio with her baby
Rhonda, who never learned to talk,
froth coming from her mouth
like sea foam.

Next door, Geraldine Riley
lived for years with all
those cats, then hanged herself
behind the front window
of her rented one-room house.
She dangled there for days
like a wilting fern, till someone
finally came and cut her down.

Margaret Parker played the piano—
was a genius, really—famous
only for being lesbian.

And one-legged Mrs. Proctor
hobbled down the road on two sticks,

had 21 kids in a three-bedroom house.
They all shit in the bathtub.
We never saw the husband.

Bobby Stringer was handsome
but never gave any of us girls
the time of day. Kenny Cooper—the boy
who used to neck with me
in the back alley—had a mother
missing a breast. He got Mary
from the chip shop pregnant.
But he liked the drink, finally died.

Margaret Waitmans wore a glass eye,
Mellie Flint had a house full of rats,
Rita Mason, a jealous husband,
who shot her for carrying on
with the milkman.

Elizabeth Larson had a clubbed foot,
she would do it with anyone
for a packet of Woodbines.

Maureen Milligan was the only girl
to go to college. Later, she died
of asthma in an ambulance.
She was the first person

I'd kissed. We'd pretended
we were boys, neither wanting
to be the girl.

Then Seed Street was bombed,
and we took in evacuees.
At night, the air raids splintered
through the night sky
like cracking bones.
We sat in the dark.

In the corner, Great Grandma Smith
held a horn to her ear, bent on an elbow,
shouting, *What? What's that?*
No one paying her any mind.

The Gift

Blackpool, England

2003

Cousin Debbie meets me
at 17 Bristol Avenue. She'll drive
me to Nanny's house, introduce
me to our grandmother.
First, she wants a picture of us
in front of the house where
our mothers grew up.
We smile for the photo.
Behind us, red and yellow
row houses lean against
each other. Narrow alleyways
lead to my mother's past.

1955

Your mum tells you you're finished
with school. You'll work
at the laundry and chip shop
off the Golden Mile.
Sundays, Mum brings
you to the Blackpool Pub.
You tell her you'd rather
stay at home with Sister Elaine,

cook the peas for supper.
Mum wants you to meet her boss.
He says a hearty hullo—face shiny,
a round balloon, a red apple.
He has seen you at the chip shop—
your knee socks, plaid skirt, girlish
lips, long brown hair. You sit
on a hard wooden stool behind
a pint of ale. He laughs wide
mouthed, throws his hands
in the air, lets one heavy hand
fall to your knee. You cough
bitter ale. The swollen fingers
fumble, the wedding ring scrapes
your thigh. You excuse yourself.
He follows you to the toilet,
closes the door behind him.
The beery breath holds
you to the wall. You concentrate
on forgetting, forgetting.
You return to the table.
He follows, smiles at your mum,
buys the table a round of drinks.
You don't say a word.
Mum says, *No need to be rude,*
a good enough bloke.
Work's not easy to come by

besides. You promise yourself
you'll leave—never return,
forget, forgotten.

2003

Nanny and I have tea and biscuits,
slide on the plastic couch cover.
She asks about Mother, touches
my face, says, *You are just like our Sheila.*
Such a shame she couldn't make it.
Then she asks, *Where are they?*
and points to the wall with her cane.
She means for me to see
my grade school photographs.
Our Sheila says you're writing
poetry. I do love poetry. Recite
us some now? No, Nanny,
I'd rather not. She crinkles
her forehead, says, *Alright then.*
Her craggy knuckles fumble
for a worn change purse.
She snaps open the clasp,
unravels a string of rhinestones,
asks, *What's this?* A necklace,
Nanny. She tucks it into the palm
of my hand, says, *A gift*
for your mother. We were like

girlfriends, you know.
Our Sheila and I,
such good friends.

Rain

Venice, Italy

At the gate of Saint Mark's Cathedral,
a dead pigeon sways in a black puddle,
mottled feathers, once wind-fluttered.

Tourists follow wooden planks across
the drenched square. The city balanced
between green canals, tilting and sinking.

In less than a year, you will have moved
out of the house, filed for divorce,
taken with you this red umbrella.

You say, *I have never seen such rain.*
The flood carries the pigeon, an eye open,
unblinking at the paper-white sky.

II. Devotion

"We do not see things as they are, we see them as we are."

—Anaïs Nin

The Syntax of Gravity

Clark Canyon, California

The tug of the rope, reminding you
that the world holds together
by the superstition of safety—
today, you won't fall. Today,
someone holds the rope below,
ready to catch you. Today,
you can defy the physics of gravity,
surrender to the chalky clouds,
the acrylic sky, the canvas of rock.
And, the rest disappears—the arms
and legs bent, then straight, hefting the weight
of their torso. The fingers and toes reaching,
uncurling, grasping, smearing, holding.
The scrape of skin against granite's lips,
the unnoticed blood. You forget even
your breath. From here, you can harness
the wind, the yellow-flowered rabbit brush,
the sage, the lodgepole pines somewhere
below. Gone is the crevice of time,
the slack monotony of what's next.
Imagination replaced by the ridge lines,
the cracks, the spine. The holds, the next
move, the quivering legs, the heart's iambic

singing. Somewhere, the distant fear
of falling. Somewhere, street children sleep
in the sewers to keep from freezing,
a leper begs on the streets. Somewhere,
a father kisses his dead son goodbye,
a soldier shoots to kill. But not here. Gone
is the world and its cold-boned grief.

Earth-Bound

Carson Pass, California

The valley unfolds before us, a white
V. The way home, and I am so tired.
For a moment, I wish I were a thing
with wings, flying from one snowy shadow
to the next, without the down, then up again.
But, there would be no crunch, slide below
my skis, a crust like wet sand. The ice stones
skittering off the shellacked edge of cliff,
swimming down the snow like a school
of slippery fish. And the carved blue
sky, clear as glass except feathery
contrails—someone always going somewhere—
and January sun, still hanging low.
Once in the sky, you can no longer see it.

A Call to Prayer

January 15, 2009

The thunder of Israeli war planes
shakes the rubble of a mosque.
The call to prayer falls
Allāhu Akbar, God is great,
through the dusty smoke.
The faithful kneel toward Mecca.
Behind them, bodies draped
with the green flags of Islam
lay on makeshift stretchers.
Some still trapped under
collapsed concrete, some
still scattered on the streets
beyond safe reach. Starving dogs
dig through the rubble. No one
should have to die this way.
Fires burn supplies in a warehouse,
bullets fall like rain. A shopkeeper
has lost both legs but still feels
the ghosts of his feet. He is propped
up by dirty blankets, stares out
at nothing. His wife sits by his side
and weeps. A family flees their home,
carrying suitcases, the white flags

of peace. They hurry along a dusty road
to nowhere. A small boy watches
as his grandmother dies in the street.
He will never forget nor forgive.
Grief is the only room—a woman
who has lost all of her children
walks into the sea.

Veiled

Old Delhi, India

The slit shows only eyes.
I know I shouldn't, but I stare
at the draped bodies, the places
where there must be mouths.

The Dinner Party

New Delhi, India

Sharma waits for us until near dawn, shivering
and smoking apricot cigarillos I gave him to relieve
my privilege. But the dinner party guests
say, Stop being so *silly*. It's a driver's *job* to wait.

I try not to think about him waiting
outside in the cold, the threadbare
double-breasted coat. The January smog
spinning around the car like a web.

Our hostess serves imported red wine
with channa masala and palak paneer. She practices
the hula hoop in the small living room. Everyone
drinks and laughs. The famous writer says

His wife has never read his books. Says he enjoys
the company of Bill Clinton as much as the Queen
of England, says you might not know it,
but Margaret Thatcher is *such* a touchy person.

The famous writer ignores my answer to his question,
more intrigued by our hostess and her hula hoop. Who
wouldn't be? No matter: I'm dazed by the 24-hour flight,

feel instead the tilt of the earth, as if I'm not really there.

Later, the writer forgets meeting me altogether.
The wife who never read his books leaves him.
Our young, lovely hostess dies suddenly. And Sharma
still sits in the cold, waiting for someone else.

Surely, something in us knows.
Like crickets singing on a log, floating
toward the waterfall, we choose to ignore
the sound of gravity.

3 AM

New Delhi, India

We stop at a streetlight. The camber of the moon appears, disappears—a white cutout in the smog. Out of the smoky night come the children—the brown irises of their eyes like dinner plates. They have emerged from their roadside tents to knock on the windows of the ambassador car. Our driver, Sharma, says, "So poor … so many so poor. What is it we can do, Ma'm. What can we do?" The children knock harder and put their hands to their mouths, miming hunger. I am afraid they may break the glass. My friend Sholeh says she wishes she had a lollipop for them. Sharma says, "Work is worship." The light turns green, the weak smiles of the children fall, and we leave them behind—ghosts of smog, still miming their hunger. Sholeh rubs her temples. I turn around, look through the window's globe, watch them disappear into the quilt of night, of smoke, of distance.

Postcard

Old Delhi, India

Motorcycles, tourist busses, camel carts, auto rickshaws, indolent cows navigate the throng of traffic. A group of children—a beautiful girl with brown, feckless eyes and smudged dirt on her cheeks, another girl with unevenly shorn hair, a small boy with a striped button-down shirt, a dirty orange sweatshirt, flimsy sandals—surrounds us. They work in teams, selling postcards, miniature carved animals. They've learned enough English to say *Postcards for your family* and *Elephants, very good luck.* Their smiles wide, ragged teeth with a yellow film. We buy books of sepia postcards. Still they follow us, holding out carved monkeys, camels, elephants. The sun shines through an aperture in the smog. We pay for the tickets to enter the sandstone walls of Shah Jahan's red fort, the backdrop of open courtyards, marble chambers, flowering mosaics. The children reach dirty fingers through the gaps between the bars.

Nothing Out of the Ordinary

Old Delhi, India

A whiskered man pulls a rickshaw through gravel.
His face, a carved totem, the lines etched
with the precision of a sharpened knife.
He is barefoot, the toenails split.
He transports a family of six. The father
carries a makeshift cage packed with live chickens.
They have plucked out their chest feathers,
revealing pink patches of skin. The mother
holds a basket with a bare-bottomed baby,
a few days old, who squirms as flies land
on her face. Her brother cups his chin in his hand,
staring out at the street—an injured cow
eating a plastic bag, a man without feet begging,
a family gathering around a small fire outside
their canvas tent. Darkness falling like ash.

In the Train Station

Varanasi, India

A turbaned man reads from the Koran.
Children beg for shampoo, food, school pens.
A boy holds his sick sister, asking
for one rupee. A teenager wants to
shine my shoes. I let him, he rips them,
offers to sew them back together
for a fee. It's not out of meanness,
but desperation. A little girl squats
on the platform. Two cows climb the stairs,
lazy as the afternoon. The train arrives.
Tourists step off. "She likes opulence,"
the husband tells their guide. "Deserves,"
she corrects him. "Well then," says the guide,
"she shall have the sky."

Spending the Night with the Dead

Varanasi, India

The first-born son has come, washed and shaved,
robed in white, circled the body, gathered the flame
eternal.

Only the unclean, the Untouchables,
may handle the dead, tend to them all hours
of the night.

The nectarine hue of smoke, a garland of flame flickers
in the night sky. A white goat noses
through the ash.

All night, Untouchables poke the flames,
cross the dirt floor, polished by bare feet,
by the heat.

Each dawn brings more saffron-wrapped
bodies, another son watching his father enter the loft
of the sky.

Another son throwing river water over
his shoulder, saying, Father, go on your way,
I'll go mine.

Three Hours to Burn a Body

Varanasi, India

I have come to watch the bodies burn,
my guide shoos away beggars and children,
selling shells of light and orange marigolds—

An offering for Mother Ganga. The murky river
sways with candles, a thousand dawn-lit stars.
The sky's stars hidden by a canvas of clouds.

Untouchables travel barefoot down sandy stairs,
carrying another gold-clad body on their shoulders.
They chant, and the families follow their dead.

I watch them tend the eternal flame, watch
the living to avoid the dead. The guide says,
"This one almost finished," points to a pyre.

A flame twists from the ghost of an eye.
"Three hours," he says, "to burn a body."
My legs hot from flame, hair rained by ash.

"Good luck," he points to the ash, "Very good luck,
indeed…Come," he leads me to a concrete building.
A creased, toothless woman holds out her hand.

A wrinkled breast sags from the sari. She tucks it back
without apology. The guide tells me, "She needs money
for her pyre. Good karma for you." I hand her 500 rupees.

She hides it in her sari, lies back onto the straw mat,
the cold concrete floor. The boatman waits. We row
down the river. Dawn prayers echo from a mosque.

A dying cow moans from the river's bank.
White branches of smoke rise from each black smudge
in the sand, disappear into the white horizon.

Children run above, along the rooftops.
Fires below create hot wind, lifting
colorful kites and children's laughter to flight.

Revision

My sister says, *Tell me about your trip,*
but don't tell me anything sad—
no hungry children and their poor
mothers, no old men hauling carts,
no street dogs, nor starving cows.

This is the gleaming Taj Mahal, built
by Mughal Emperor Shah Jahan
for his queen, a marble memorial
of love. The semi-precious stones
burn in the moonlight like secrets.

After 22 years of building the mausoleum,
Shah Jahan cut off the hands of the artisans.
Without their hands, they could never betray
him by replicating the intricate stone mosaics.

The Taj Mahal shines in the city of Agra,
attracting millions of tourists each year
from all over the world.

Crooked-backed women and bony cows sift
through the dunes of smoking garbage,
searching for something to eat. Our driver Sharma

points to the mountains of trash, says
"Welcome to Agra." A small boy drags along
the litter-strewn street on his knees and his elbows,
limbs crumpled like broken wings.

This is Old Delhi's Red Fort,
built in the original city of Shahjahanabad.
The sandstone walls and turrets
have weathered the centuries.

Plastic tarps serve as homes in the center divider
of Old Delhi's highway. Families huddle
around bonfires, the weak flickering,
a yellow glow in January's damp smog.
Children sell trinkets on the crowded streets,
the barefoot girl with ragged hair, the eyes
bottomless brown pools.

Varanasi is a holy city, the River Ganga
is worshipped as a goddess. It is said
cremation in Varanasi means release
from the karmic cycle of life.

The dog wasn't killed, only maimed,
outside Varanasi's Buddhist temple.
The bump under the tire was followed
by the cry, shrill like ice. The driver's shrug—

the pack of dogs circling the car, barking

in lamentation for the crushed hip,

the body's revision, the leg

now a dangling ghost.

The Nearly Dead

Varanasi, India

Dusk catches the world in its gauzy net.
The sun hangs like a ripe tangerine
behind the smoke. Rafts loaded with wood
travel the Ganges. A blind man follows us,
selling cotton candy, the pink poufs electric
against the gray water, the darkening sky.
We buy the candy for the children. They fight
over the pink wisps, then surround us,
begging for more, for rupees, school pens.
Our guide shoos them away—they run off
to find another game, their laughter ringing
like bells. They take turns sliding down
the ghat steps on an old piece of cardboard.
The nearly dead slump at the bottom
of the stairs, asking for pyre money,
hoping to afford a complete cremation.
The carriage of their hips, blackened skulls
not flung in the river nearly whole,
but rendered to dust. The world itself
unveiled, made bare.

The Road

Varanasi, India

We huddle in the backseat
of the ambassador car, breathe
into our shawls, the smoke burning
our noses and throats, our eyes.
Behind us, a cart full of concrete bags
pulled by an old man on a bicycle.
Next to us, an insouciant camel
hauling a load of wood.
In front of us, an SUV with a body
tied to the luggage rack. A foot
peeks out from underneath
the shimmering orange fabric
of the death gown. The ball of the foot,
gleaming white in the smoggy light.
It feels like this should be private,
the creases of toes, the chalky heel,
the hummock of an ankle. The single foot
like a stranger's secret I overhear in passing.

Along the Ganges

Varanasi, India

Three small girls want to sell me shells filled with marigolds
and candles to set afloat on Mother Ganga, an offering of light,
karma, prosperity. The promise of a wish come true.

They hold their baskets at their sides, stand barefoot
at the edge of the river. I photograph them,
and they smile at their digital images, reach for the camera.

I motion for them to pose together, but they refuse.
The taller girl, the one with some English, explains
that the other girls are Dalits, Untouchables.

She can't stand with them for the photograph, so I take a picture
of the two together, then the bigger girl alone. I reach down, set
my shell on the Ganges, but the shell flips, the flame flickers and dies.

The Sacred

Aleppy, India

The flare of cricket song burns into the night,
the rooster's answer to the darkness,
to the light. The veined wind shakes the reeds,
and lanterns sway against a southern sky.
Two men saunter hand in hand, smile at me,
say, *Hello*, then ask, *What is your country?*

Women wearing saris and flip-flops move earth
to metal tins with bent shovels, They carry rocks
on their heads. Children beg, *One school pen?*
Please? They play games with coconuts,
swing from palm fronds, turn cartwheels
on the sand, splash into the Arabian Sea.

Walk along the shore, through the rice paddies,
into your own malaria dreams. Give
a leper food, unwrap it for him. Touch
the stone of the temple before you enter,
3,000 years of looking forward, looking back.

Tour Bus

Beijing, China

Where's the bathroom/Where
is a proper toilet/I couldn't possibly/
How much does it cost/I was overcharged/
I don't understand this money/How much
is a dollar/Can't you just take American dollars/
I can't sleep/I would like six appointments
in the next two days/A facial, nails, hair,
and three massages/Is the tip included/
Why doesn't anyone speak English/
Where is the market/This isn't like home/
I have lost my way/Can you take me
to the St. Regis Hotel on your rickshaw/
Why don't you speak English/Where
is the Starbucks/Where is the Forbidden City/
What is so forbidden about it/Whose tomb
is that/What did he do/ Should I take a picture/
Will you take a picture/Press hard/No
look through here/See/Here/Hard/
What is the Way/I don't understand/
You don't understand/Isn't there
any American food/Like a hamburger/
Or spaghetti/Are these really snails/
I couldn't possibly.

The Hutong

Beijing, China

Small shops sell pencils, rice,
haircuts, quivering prawns, rusting
car parts, green snails, still flopping
fish. Red lanterns and caged parakeets
hang along alleyways. The street corners
house public toilets and telephones.

A bare-chested man in pajama bottoms
works bent over a bicycle,
replacing the split rubber tube.
Women swish fingers through plastic
tubs of squid, making their selections.

Bicycles, rickshaws, motorcycles,
old women pulling carts, men
pushing wheelbarrows weave past.
Two blocks away, glass high rises
form elegant curves, sharp angles,
reflecting a smog-pleated sky.

Shops line the streets—
Bally, Tiffany & Co, Nike,
Polo, and Gucci. Diamonds,

cashmere, the latest silk fashions.

A billboard shows a jet slicing

through a cloudless blue sky.

Next to the Chinese letters,

the English reads *London*

has never been so close.

The Mongolian Disco

Ulaanbaatar, Mongolia

The children of diplomats
drink and smoke, hide behind
mirrored sunglasses. Scantily-clad
women teeter by in stilettos, glitter
in strobe lights, vibrate to the beat of trance.
Cocktail waitresses head upstairs
to the VIP-only balcony,
they carry round platters of Red Bull,
Genghis Khan vodka, fire sparklers.
Their legs glow in the neon light.
The white leather couch is reserved
for one man. It must be that the real
Genghis Khan is buried around here
somewhere. His bones rattle in the earth.
We share his name, eat it for all these years.

Throat Singing

Ulaanbaatar, Mongolia

The animal in the stomach
wakes, trembles, and crawls
to the chest. The voice
in a cave, a wind tunnel.
The guttural slither into the horn
of the throat, vibrating, leaving
a body, entering mine.

Devotion

Ulaanbaatar, Mongolia

The morning chants echo from the Gandan Monastery.
I approach the old monk. He is to read my sutras.
He takes both hands, turns the palms up.
Incense and sweat hang in the air. The monks silence
their chants, break for a bowl of porridge.
The old monk looks at me through tinted glasses,
says something. I look to the translator, she tells me,
"He says he can tell you, but only after you understand.
After more attention to your true work. Only then,
you must return." He nods, turns to go, his maroon
and yellow robes sweep the floor. Outside the gates,
a homeless woman crouches on the street,
scooping rain water from the gutter into a thermos.
Old women offer small bottles of ablution.
Street children wearing plastic sandals,
their dirty socks drenched, sell bird seed, beg
for spare change. Mist falls now a steady rain,
pigeons lift into the cloud-pleated sky, the chants resume—
the flutter, the rain, the boundlessness of human song.

About the Author

Suzanne Roberts is the author of two previous collections of poetry, *Shameless* (Cherry Grove Collections, 2007) and *Nothing to You* (Pecan Grove Press, 2008). She was named "The Next Great Travel Writer" by National Geographic's *Traveler*. She holds a doctorate in Literature and the Environment from the University of Nevada-Reno and currently writes and teaches in South Lake Tahoe, California. For more information, please visit her website at www.suzanneroberts.org.

CPSIA information can be obtained at www.ICGtesting.com
Printed in the USA
BVOW011545140911

271195BV00002B/22/P

9 781936 370375